The Transformation of Dr. Ugs

John Forlenza-Bailey, M.Ed., LADC

The Reading Glass Books
1-888-420-3050
www.readingglassbooks.com
fulfillment@readingglassbooks.com

Table of Contents

Author's Note

The Transformation of Dr.Ugs is an original story that explains the progression of the disease of chemical dependency. It is not intended to be a story about blaming others for the acquisition of an illness. This story is intended to explain not to blame. It is a story of discovery, insight, acceptance, and finally the right choices to live drug free if one is Chemically Dependent.

The story begins with an introduction to the Ugs family after the only son is born. His name is Harry. The story is deeply rooted in metaphors and Harry signifies "worry" or "trouble." Harry (H.Ugs) becomes Dr.Ugs as drinking and drugging become a problem for him. He loses touch with his sisters Faith, Hope, and Charity, and his communication with his parents is lost.

Parenting was mostly assumed by Harry's mother – much too difficult a task for one parent. Harry's father's time was very limited due to the priority of providing for the Ugs family. Harry has received wounds in his childhood and young adulthood such as child abuse, abandonment, jealousy, lost first love, and chemical dependency.

Throughout the story Dr.Ugs is feared and his behavior and attitude become very frightening. Drugging and drinking consequences became more and more severe until a moment of truth caused a transformation. The miracle of answered prayers is suggested as the reason for the transformation, and Dr.Ugs becomes "Hugs not Drugs" and he has become free from substance abuse via daily reprieve based on a spiritual way of life.

"Hugs not Drugs" has three friends, Will Power, Dr. Eams (aka dreams), and Old Max Simms. They are his role models because they provide "Hugs not Drugs" with emotional support and education at the end of the story. The metaphors throughout the story are meant to be entertaining as well as descriptive. Although the subject matter is grim; the format is filled with humor, inspiration, and upbeat intents.

The Transformation of Dr. Ugs

Mr. and Mrs. Ugs had four children. First came Faith, then came Hope, then came Harry, and then came Charity. Mr. Ugs was a hard working man. Papa Ugs needed to provide for his family, so he worked and was away from home quite a bit. Mrs. Ugs was left to provide nurturing for her children. This was difficult to do.

When Harry was born, it was a proud day for the Ugs parents. They were happy Mama Ugs already had two children so she knew how to care for an infant. Harry seemed to get special treatment. It seemed he did not want anything. Harry had two sisters to watch him and a Mama who gave him plenty of time and attention. Harry rested and played. He looked very content. As a toddler, he would just need to point and say the word "Ug," and he would get anything that he wanted. Saying, "Ug" would get him food. Saying "Ug, Ug" would get Harry out of his swing. "Ug, Ug, Ug" would get his diaper changed. There seemed to be an "Ug" interpretation for anything he wished.

Harry was the little prince of the Ugs household.

Finally, after seven years of "Ugging" little Harry learned to master a more sophisticated language - English. Harry did not like being more ordinary. He loved the attention of being special. During this time, Charity was born. This was quite an adjustment for Harry, and he did not do well with it. Harry's world with Faith and Hope was tolerable, but living with Charity, Harry found this difficult. Harry was less and less the royal one. No more "Ugging" - that ship had sailed.

But, Harry being Harry, he tried to return to "Ugging." However, Mama Ugs was having none of that regression. Mama Ugs was the only parent around for child rearing most of the time, and it was frustrating and difficult to single parent four children. The corporal punishment of slapping was something that Mama Ugs learned at her home growing up with her own brother and sister years before.

Mama Ugs grew up in a toxic environment due to her father'salcoholism. Mama Ugs' father drank to excess on a regular basis. His name was Justin A'Nono. Justin A'Nono would drink and then he would like to fight. Hitting family members was a regular occurrence for Justin A'Nono. Mama Ugs learned to hit from her family. In fact, slapping was something that was done regularly by Mama Ugs' ancestors for many generations.

Multi-generational Cycles of Abuse

4

Of course there was the physical pain after a slapping, but the more hurtful and lasting was the emotional pain. Physical pain would go away; emotional pain kept building up and did not go away. With very little child rearing help from Papa Ugs, Mama Ugs was worn out. Frustration and anger were the emotions behind little Harry getting hit.

Harry started preparing for the hitting. If he walked by his mother and he was unsure of her disposition (which was most of the time) Harry would put his head down and duck. This looked very funny to Mama Ugs and sometimes she would laugh.

Other times she would be insulted by Harry's ducking and Harry would receive slaps for his preparing for slaps. This was a sad time for Harry.

The Ugs Family liked to go to church. Harry liked church since age seven when he started drinking the communion wine. In fact, Harry became a regular altar server from age 7 to age 19 drinking communion wine all the while. It was a way to feel good when Harry went through his sad and disenchanted times. He did well in school in spite of his imbibing in the communion wine. The major consequence for Harry when drinking for these 12 years was that he evolved into a dishonest, selfish, and willful young man instead of an honest, open, and willing young man.

Harry was a loner, and became more and more disenchanted. He was growing up and was expected to learn how to get things in life without saying all those "Ugs." Harry thought to himself, "All this life experience and I still cannot get what I want — "Ug." Harry learned not to trust others, talk to others, identify feelings, ask questions, or think for fear of being disappointed by others - "Ug." Harry was conditioned to these habits and they were the only survival skills that he learned in the Ugs household.

Harry thought he found the solution to his problem -
Drinking and drugging through the ages

Then one day Harry Ugs met Ms. Perception. It was love at first sight. Ms. Perception saw Harry and the feeling was mutual.

Harry Ugs' nickname – H.Ugs was given to him by Ms Perception. H.Ugs fell in love with Ms. Perception when he was 19 years old. H.Ugs did not need the communion wine or the church for that matter when he was in love. So he unceremoniously left the church and was less and less involved with family or friends. Ms. Perception was his one and only or better known as 'The One.'

Ms. Perception gave Harry his nickname, H.Ugs

Unfortunately for H.Ugs Ms. Perception did not love Harry after their torrid summer of love. Ms. Perception wanted space from H.Ugs and told him so at the end of their summer romance in no uncertain terms. H.Ugs could not handle this truth. H.Ugs was heartbroken.

In order to feel good, H.Ugs resumed drinking alcohol and using lots of different drugs. During this time friends and family renamed H.Ugs to Dr.Ugs. That name Dr.Ugs was to be his nickname for the next 10 years.

It is important to note that when Dr.Ugs started drinking and drugging, those old survival skills made him feel wonderful. Dr.Ugs did not understand that alcohol and drugs had historically always been a huge problem in the Ugs family. It was confusing, because drinking and drugging made him feel good, but there would be consequences later. Dr.Ugs became blind to the sane and sound world just like some of his ancestors. Soon he had hardly anything to do with Faith, Hope, Charity, Mama, or Papa Ugs.

Dr.Ugs got sicker – physically, emotionally, and spiritually. Socially, he became an outcast. He had no friends, and people that knew him were afraid of him. The sicker Dr.Ugs became; the more frightening he became. His Ugs family survival skills of not talking, not feeling, not trusting seemed impossible to break. Dr.Ugs would tell anyone who would listen that the reason he drank and drugged was to help mend a broken heart. He would explain that he fell in love with Ms. Perception. He loved her so much and she loved him. He wanted to get his physical, emotional, and spiritual needs met with Ms. Perception. The same easy way he got his needs met by saying the word "Ug." But, it was not to be. Dr.Ugs did not know that it was impossible for another human being to fulfill someone's physical, emotional, and spiritual needs. Dr.Ugs was delusional.

H.Ugs was lost in the search to fill these needs, and Dr.Ugs evolved. This conflict, frustration, and void led to a life where Dr.Ugs could not identify what he felt. His thinking became very muddled and unclear. Dr.Ugs' behavior was not accepted by his family or friends. Even people who drank and drugged would not befriend him.

Dr.Ugs went to many hospitals. His diagnosis by the doctors was – "CHRONIC AND INCURABLE UGLINESS" as evidenced by his inability to live life on life's terms. It was a very strange time.

How strange was it? It was so strange that if Dr.Ugs did acquire a friendship then it would end up 'Ugly' within twenty-four hours. It was so strange that all his so-called girlfriends, when he was fortunate to get a date, had the same name - they were all Ms. Conceptions. To know Dr.Ugs was not to love Dr.Ugs.

They would leave the company of Dr.Ugs within a short period of time. It was truly amazing how many Ms. Conceptions would be found by Dr.Ugs when he was looking for a relationship. The results were predictable. Dr.Ugs would get – ugly.

Dr.Ugs had many Ms. Conceptions

It seems that Dr.Ugs' days kept getting worse, never better. Dr.Ugs was on a downward spiral. Consequences of this spiral were:

- No memory of things after a night of drinking and drugging;
- Dr.Ugs would have negative feelings without drinking.
- Dr.Ugs would get GAS in his heart, that is Guilt, Anger, and Shame. And, the way it was relieved was to get high so Dr.Ugs could not sense the GAS;
- No real employment opportunities. A job was always left eventually due to "ugly" conditions;
- Several years of depression. At one point, Dr.Ugs lay on the Ugs family couch for two years watching television, eating, sleeping a lot, and taking medication for his diagnosis of "Ugly";
- Dr.Ugs was pitied, feared, and made fun of;
- Dr.Ugs was lonely;
- Dr.Ugs' social skills continued to get worse;
- Dr.Ugs would steal, lie, and cheat to drink and drug;
- Dr.Ugs did not like anyone, especially himself; and
- Dr.Ugs tried to kill himself with drugs and alcohol, but all attempts continued to fail. Situations kept getting uglier.

The vicious cycle ended with an ill prepared trip to NYC. Dr.Ugs was on his way to becoming a great actor. Without any money or talent, just lots of delusional thinking, he set off in his bucket of bolts of a car. During his journey, Dr.Ugs was informed by the New Jersey State Troopers to get off the toll road due to his lack of funding. It was another delusional day for Dr.Ugs as his journey left him arriving naked in a police station early one November Saturday Morning in a beach community in New Jersey. It was not the first time Dr.Ugs did something outrageous like this although the nakedness was a first. He went through delirium tremors while waiting in a jail cell. While this was a new low, being transferred to another residential hospital was a pattern.

This was not the first time he had done something crazy making people afraid of him. It was not the first time he had to stand in line for his mashed potatoes. It was not the first time he was beaten for causing a disturbance. Nor was it the first time he visually and auditorily hallucinated that he was the "Messiah for Mankind."

It was a vicious downward spiral

After a series of misadventures, and the latest residence change, something different happened. Dr. Ugs asked for help by calling his father, Papa Ugs. He kept repeating in a very defeated way to Papa Ugs, "I'M CRAZY AND I'M CHEMICALLY DEPENDENT, AND I WANT HELP."

Dr. Ugs was transformed by the simple gesture of asking for help.

As if by magic, internally in the brain and the heart, everything was different. The transformation of Dr. Ugs had happened by becoming aware of his drinking and drugging and asking for help. Physical, Emotional, and Spiritual Pain had become the touchstone for the pursuit of transformation. Harry Ugs had his Spiritual Transformation!

Papa Ugs, although he felt helpless about losing Harry and gaining Dr. Ugs, had been praying with Mama Ugs for many years that their son would return to them. Mama and Papa had learned long ago to detach with love due to their own prayer lives.

Dr. Ugs appeared to be transformed by asking for help and the Ugs' family prayers had been answered. From seemingly out of nowhere, they heard their son on the phone call say, "Maybe I have a problem with drugs and alcohol. I'm sick and tired of being sick and tired."

Papa Ugs went to pick up Harry out of the hospital. He traveled over 200 miles. When Papa Ugs arrived, he found Harry instead of Dr. Ugs. Harry kept repeating how he wanted something different. Harry vowed, "I'll not be Dr. Ugs even if I have to say it out loud every five minutes."

Papa Ugs saw the same determination he used to see from his little infant, the toddler, then pre-school Harry when he would say "Ug" and Papa Ugs knew just what little Harry was saying. In recovery Harry Ugs received a new nickname that he hoped to keep for the rest of his life. That nickname was "Hugs Not Drugs."

The Transformation from Dr.Ugs to H.Ugs

It had taken many years for the transformation of Dr. Ugs to "Hugs Not Drugs" to occur and the transformation only happened based on a physical, emotional, and spiritual conditioning that occurs "One Day at a Time" (ODAAT). Instead of avoiding physical, emotional, and or spiritual pain, "Hugs Not Drugs" learned that pain is the touchstone of physical, emotional, and spiritual growth.

Years before "The Transformation of Hugs Not Drugs" he remembered that he would attend self help groups telling people he wanted help, but it was a lie, a sad con job. He remembered thinking he wasn't that bad. However, during the phone call to Papa Ugs and after this spiritual awakening, "Hugs not Drugs" concluded he was worse than most of the stories he had heard, and now he wanted to recover from his addiction. He made a vow to God that when he left the hospital, he committed to being "Hugs Not Drugs."

"Hugs Not Drugs" learned many lessons. Mainly that the only way to heal pain was to go through it, not around it with resentment, remorse, and reservations. And, when doing that he learned that living life on life's terms and taking the spiritual path instead of the "psycho path" took Courage and Humility.

"Hugs Not Drugs" now understands that involvement with others in the Good Orderly Direction Groups he regularly attends is better than his way as Dr. Ugs. He now understands that the enemy, Dr. Ugs, still resides inside of him. "Hugs Not Drugs" knows his true enemy. "Hugs Not Drugs" combs that enemy's hair in the morning.

However, he now doesn't try to kill the enemy, he only loves and educates the enemy with love and forgiveness to the best of his ability on a daily basis. The transformation of Dr. Ugs is ongoing. There is no end to enlightenment for "Hugs Not Drugs" as he stays motivated and works to keep his recovery skills healthy.

While attending his recovery meetings, something wonderful happened, "Hugs Not Drugs" met three close friends, Will Power, Dr. Eams (Dreams), and Old Max Simms. They became his best friends in the Good Orderly Direction Groups that "Hugs not Drugs" attended regularly.

Will Power is a famous professional athlete. Many children have made Will Power their hero. When Will Power first met "Hugs not Drugs," he told him, "When I, Will Power, drank and drugged, it nearly destroyed my ability to be the hero to all my fans - I lost. When I booze, I lose, it's that simple." He continued, "It looks like we both need to stay clean and sober, one day at a time. We can have that goal and do this together."

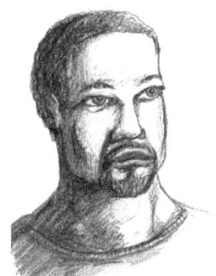

Will Power

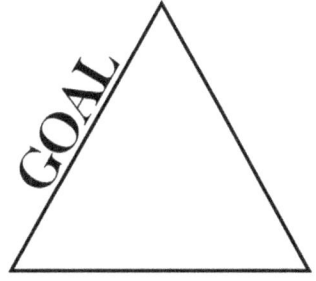

You need a Goal

Dr. Eams and Old Max Simms were in earshot of Will Power's remarks to "Hugs not Drugs." Dr. Eams echoed Will Power's sentiment by saying, "Hugs not Drugs", there is no doubt in my mind that I, Dr. Eams needs, wants, and would love you to be my friend. When I was a slave to those street drugs, pharmaceuticals, and drinking, I looked like a twin to Dr.Ugs. I was lonely and did not have the capacity to be true to myself. But now, after lots of self discovery, since I don't drink and or do drugs, I am true to myself, and can follow my bliss."

Dr. Eams identified with "Hugs not Drugs," inability to trust others, talk out problems or find solutions realistically. He shared, "My brain chemistry was very distorted when I was active. I was dangerous. However, now I know, the monster will wake up when I think negatively and don't process feelings appropriately. I have to remember to take my goal, develop a plan and review it daily so I can make my dreams come true!"

Dr. Eams

Your Goal needs a Plan

Old Max Simms heard laughing and joined the conversation, "If we don't stand for something, we will fall for anything." I think Malcolm X said that! "We need to hang together, or we will hang separately." I think Benjamin Franklin said that. "I cannot do it alone, together we can, one day at a time, first things first, and with an easy does it attitude. Well you know me, I can go on forever," said old Max Simms.

The others nodded. They agreed with Old Max Simms. What he was saying was true. They identified. Old Max Simms could carry on a conversation all by himself if it were necessary for him to stay sober and clean. Even though the group may tire of his rhetoric, his sayings contained wisdom that usually helped center "Hugs not Drugs" to remain vigilant to the primary strategy of staying in recovery. Recovering people usually agree that Old Max Simms has wisdom.

Old Max Simms

And when you add Wisdom
You have HOPE

Old Max Simms concluded, "Make no military mistake about it —- Drugs are not cool for some people. Hugs are better than Drugs. – Amen. I am not the man I want to be, but thank God I am not the man I used to be."

"Hugs not Drugs", Will Power, Dr. Eams and Old Max Simms, traveled the road to wellness together and their relationship deepend through the years. "Hugs not Drugs" knows the enemy can wake up and take over if he forgets who he is, but through the interdependence of these friends, he now helps others recover to a healthy lifestyle.

"Hugs Not Drugs" attending A Good Orderly Direction Meeting

Epilogue

This story is ending with the inside joke that "They all Lived Happily Ever After." Recovery is like a beautiful swan swimming across the river. However, underneath the water, the swan is paddling with all of its strength and agility to keep moving.

People in recovery make mistakes, but they understand that mistakes are blessings. Mistakes empower the transformation of recovery to continue. "Hugs Not Drugs" has learned that although we make mistakes, none of us are a mistake.

Remember love and forgiveness are the answers to any question. "The Transformation of Dr.Ugs" is real. Relax and trust the process. You are worth it!

THE END

Old Maxims
Learned after 45 years of recovery

- Love is the answer, whatever the question
- Awareness, Admission, Acceptance, and Action are keys to self reflection to stay away from the first drink or drug
- The surest way to humility is humiliation
- The program works if you believe in God, the program works if you don't believe in God, the program won't work if you believe you are God
- Gratitude is an action word. Don't tell me you are grateful, show me.
- I'm helping you because you help me
- I only need two meetings a week to be sober and serene. I go to seven because I don't know which two they are
- I go to meetings to find out what will happen if I don't go to meetings
- If you don't stand for something you'll fall for anything
- I love you all the time; not your behavior some of the time
- I will not validate invalid behavior
- Seven days without a meeting makes one weak
- Motivation plus skill equals success
- If you want to drink or drug, don't use, call me first, and if it's a good enough reason, I'll buy (just kidding)

- There are 4 "A's" to recovery - awareness, admission, acceptance, and action
- When all else fails, follow directions
- Everywhere I go, there I am
- Fear knocked on the door, faith answered, fear was gone
- If you pray why worry, if you worry, why pray
- The only way to deal with something is to deal with it
- The G's of recovery - God, Guts, Get Up and Go, and Gratitude
- "Action" is the magic word in recovery
- 3 R's of Relapse - Resentment, Remorse, and Reservations
- HALT - don't get Hungry, Angry, Lonely, or Tired
- ODAAT - One Day at a Time
- There's no end to enlightenment
- DENIAL - Don't Even Know I am Lying
- The truth will set you free but first it will make you angry
- Recovery is one big 'let go,' unfortunately whatever I let go of usually has claw marks
- Attitude plus behavior equals consequences
- I am powerless of over people, places, and things

Special Thanks

Alcoholics Anonymous, New York, World Services, Inc., 1939

Chemically Dependent Anonymous, Severna Park, MD, General Service Office, 1990

Editor and Contributor of Ms. Conceptions Artwork (Artist Unknown) Anna Forlenza-Bailey, 2025 (a princess)

Image Artist: Joe Guillette, 2025 (a prince)

Reading Glass Bookstores' Staff, especially Sonia Martinez, Wrightstown, NJ 2025

Road to Wellness Workbook, Red Bank, NJ, Newman Springs Publishing, 2018

In Memory

John L. and Dorothy Bailey
Harry and Jane Forlenza

Some of the characters in this story were created by my wonderful brother-in-law, John D. White. John White created the character Dr. Ugs and Will Power in 1988. I loved the creations so much that I asked John if I could write a story and create more characters. This story is dedicated to him and to all my family and friends in Twelve Step Recovery. You are all wonderful inspirations.

About the Author

John Forlenza-Bailey is a substance abuse professional for over 40 years. He is the author of "The Road to Wellness Workbook" and lives in Bloomfield, Connecticut with his wonderful wife, Anna Forlenza-Bailey. They raised two great men/musicians - Harry and Zachary Forlenza-Bailey.

John Forlenza-Bailey can be contacted at johnforlenzabailey@gmail.com
Or at: Psychology Today/John Forlenza-Bailey
Chemical Addictions Treatment Services (CATS)

To hear more from John, check out The Hugs Not Drugs Podcast. Search for it exactly as written, The Hugs Not Drugs Podcast, to discover how this podcast supports motivated individuals in recovery with tools and insights for personal growth.